One Crazy Summer

Rita Williams-Garcia

TEACHER GUIDE

NOTE:

The trade book edition of the novel used to prepare this guide is found in the Novel Units catalog and on the Novel Units website. Using other editions may have varied page references.

Please note: We have assigned Interest Levels based on our knowledge of the themes and ideas of the books included in the Novel Units sets, however, please assess the appropriateness of this novel or trade book for the age level and maturity of your students prior to reading with them. You know your students best!

SBN 978-1-60878-724-1

rinted in the United States of America.

To order, contact your local school supply store, or:

Toll-Free Fax: 877.716.7272
Phone: 888.650.4224
3901 Union Blvd., Suite 155
St. Louis, MO 63115

sales@novelunits.com

novelunits.com

Table of Contents

Summary....................3

About the Author....................3

Characters....................4

Background Information....................5

Initiating Activities....................6

Vocabulary Activities....................6

Eight Sections....................7
Each section contains: Summary, Vocabulary, Discussion Questions, and Supplementary Activities

Post-reading Discussion Questions....................23

Post-reading Extension Activities....................26

Assessment....................27

Scoring Rubric....................36

Skills and Strategies

Critical Thinking
Analysis, research, evaluation, interpretation, compare/contrast, drawing conclusions

Comprehension
Inferring, sequencing, predicting, supporting judgments

Literary Elements
Point of view, setting, theme, genre, figurative language, character analysis

Vocabulary
Definitions, word maps, target words, parts of speech

Listening/Speaking
Discussion, report, interview, recitation

Writing
Interview, letter, poetry, essay, short description, personal narrative

Across the Curriculum
Social Studies—Oakland, Black Panther Party, Civil Rights Movement, COINTELPRO, Cassius Clay (Muhammad Ali), Eldridge Cleaver, Huey Newton, Afros, Bobby Hutton, Gwendolyn Brooks, resistance movement publications; Geography—maps; Art—illustration, scrapbook

Genre: historical fiction

Setting: the summer of 1968 in Oakland, California

Point of View: first person

Themes: family, sisterhood, motherhood, civil rights, dignity, personal freedom, integration, prejudice, injustice, responsibility

Conflict: person vs. person, person vs. society

Style: narrative

Tone: conversational, informative

Date of First Publication: 2010

Summary

Eleven-year-old Delphine narrates the story of her and her two younger sisters' month-long visit to Oakland, California to visit their mother, Cecile. They have been estranged from Cecile since she left the family seven years prior, just after Fern, the youngest daughter, was born. Cecile is a poet and greatly resents the intrusion of the children into her life, so she sends them to the People's Center, a Black Panther organization for young people. Initially, the girls are upset because of their mother's negligence, as they must navigate through the unfamiliar environment by themselves. However, as they make friends and contribute to the Black Panthers' pursuit of justice and equality, they begin to enjoy themselves. As the girls learn more about their mother, they gradually form a bond with her.

About the Author

Rita Williams-Garcia was born in Queens, New York in 1957. She and her two siblings grew up in Seaside, California, where her father served in the army. She began to read at an early age and displayed an interest in writing throughout her childhood. Her family moved back to New York when Williams-Garcia was in high school. She attended Hofstra University and obtained a job at a marketing company after college, which allowed her to type, print, and send her manuscripts to publishing companies. Williams-Garcia published her first novel, *Blue Tights*, in 1988. Other novels include *Every Time a Rainbow Dies, Fast Talk on a Slow Track, Like Sisters on the Homefront,* and *No Laughter Here*, all of which were chosen as ALA Best Books for Young Adults. She received a 2011 Newbery Honor, Coretta Scott King Award, and Scott O'Dell Award for Historical Fiction for *One Crazy Summer*. She has also won the PEN/Norma Klein Award and was a National Book Award Finalist. Williams-Garcia currently lives in Jamaica, New York and is on the faculty at the Vermont College of Fine Arts in the Writing for Children & Young Adults Program.

Characters

Delphine Gaither: 11-year-old girl who is responsible for her two younger sisters; mature and caring; narrates the story

Vonetta Gaither: nine-year-old girl; outgoing and attention-seeking; loves to perform; often bullies Fern and allows others to also

Fern (Afua) Gaither: seven-year-old girl; attached to her white baby doll, Miss Patty Cake; courageous and outspoken

Louis Gaither ("Pa"): Delphine, Vonetta, and Fern's father; sends the girls to Oakland, California to meet their mother for the first time

Big Ma: Louis's mother; an old-fashioned, Southern black woman who was frequently at odds with Cecile; has taken care of the girls since their mother left

Darnell Gaither: Louis's younger brother who is away fighting in Vietnam; used to recount memories of Cecile with Delphine

Cecile (Nzila): Delphine, Vonetta, and Fern's mother; abandoned her daughters; moved to California to be a poet; inattentive to the girls when they visit; supports the Black Panthers

"Mean Lady" Ming: owner of the Chinese restaurant the girls frequent in California

"Crazy" Kelvin: militant member of the Black Panthers; teases the girls with his strong opinions and his criticism of Fern's white baby doll; police informant

Sister Mukumbu: teacher at the People's Center; involves the Gaither girls in Black Panther activities; warm and welcoming

Sister Pat: young woman who works at the People's Center

Eunice, Janice, and Beatrice Ankton: three sisters who go to the People's Center; become close friends with Delphine, Vonetta, and Fern

Hirohito Woods: both African-American and Japanese; loves to ride his go-kart; His father was arrested for being a "freedom fighter."

Mrs. Woods: Hirohito's mother; cares for the girls after Cecile is arrested

Background Information

1. **Oakland, California**—Oakland is where the Black Panther Party originated. The relationship between the Gaither girls and their mother is the main focus of the novel, but Williams-Garcia surrounds that story with an exploration of the Civil Rights Movement and the themes of injustice, prejudice, and black pride, as reflected through Black Panther ideals.

2. **1968**—As the Vietnam War raged on, protests and disturbances occurred on a number of campuses, including the University of Wisconsin, the University of North Carolina, and Howard University. In April, Martin Luther King, Jr. was assassinated, followed by Robert F. Kennedy in June. Also, unrest arose in Cleveland with a shootout between police officers and a number of African-American men. In Oakland, young Black Panther Bobby Hutton was killed by the police. The Democratic National Convention also resulted in clashes between police and protestors.

3. **Black Panther Party**—The Black Panther Party was founded by Huey Newton and Bobby Seale in Oakland, California in 1966. Black Panthers wore blue shirts, black pants, black leather jackets, and black berets. The group's primary purpose was to protect African-American neighborhoods from police brutality. They instituted a program called "Free Breakfast for Children" and advanced a political agenda concerned with employment, housing, and education. However, the organization became infamous both nationally and internationally for its aggressiveness against police officers. FBI Director J. Edgar Hoover supervised a program called "COINTELPRO" to weaken the party's threat and influence in the United States. The program used tactics such as perjury, infiltration, surveillance, and police harassment to achieve its goals. In 1967, Huey Newton was jailed for killing an Oakland police officer, which led to the "Free Huey" campaign, during which people painted posters to show their support, just as the girls do in the novel. Bobby Hutton, a 17-year-old Black Panther, was memorialized after he was killed in an ambush against the police. Although he had surrendered and proved he was unarmed, Hutton was shot to death by officers. In 1969, Black Panther membership reached a peak of 10,000 but began to decline throughout the 1970s and 1980s.

Initiating Activities

Use one or more of the following to introduce the novel.

1. Writing: Have students respond to the following writing prompt: If you could change one thing in the world, what would it be? Explain your choice.
2. Research: Have students complete the I Have Heard of... activity on page 28 of this guide.
3. Locate Information: Preview the novel with students, discussing the author, the title's meaning, and the cover illustration.
4. Brainstorming/Art: Have students define a mother's role in a child's life and draw a picture portraying their definition. Then, have students explain their drawings.
5. Predictions: Have students complete the I Predict... activity on page 29 of this guide.

Vocabulary Activities

1. Bingo: Give each student a 5×5 grid and a set of 24 vocabulary words. Have them place the words randomly on their grids, leaving the center space as a "free" spot. A caller chooses definition cards from a pile, and students place markers on the words the definitions match. The first student to get five words in a row—horizontally, vertically, or diagonally—calls out "Bingo!" The winner can call the next game.
2. Word Maps: Have students complete a Word Map (see page 30 of this guide) for six vocabulary words from this guide.
3. Target Word Story: Instruct students to write an original short story using the following vocabulary words from the lists in this guide: pry, fugitive, refrained, documenting, defiant, gesturing, clumsy. Students should highlight the vocabulary words they use in their stories.
4. Vocabulary Memory: Using 3×5 index cards, have students work in pairs to write words on one set of cards and definitions on another set. Lay all of the cards face down on a desk. Students should then play the Memory Game, turning over cards and trying to match words with their correct definitions. If a student finds a match, he or she should pick up those cards and take another turn. If there is no match, the turn goes to the next player. Play continues until all the cards have been matched, and the player with the most matches wins.
5. Glossary: Ask students to keep a list of any unfamiliar or difficult words they encounter as they read the novel. Have students create a glossary from their lists. Glossaries should include each word's pronunciation, part of speech, and definition as it is used in the novel.

Cassius Clay Clouds–Green Stucco House

Three sisters—Delphine Vonetta, and Fern—travel on an airplane from Brooklyn, New York to Oakland, California to see their mother Cecile for the first time since she abandoned them seven years ago. Delphine, the eldest daughter and the novel's narrator, takes responsibility for her younger sisters on their journey. Cecile is late arriving at the airport and shows little interest in the girls. She walks ahead of them, makes them hold their luggage in the taxi, and unceremoniously brings them to her green stucco house.

Vocabulary
whimper pry surging warbled uppity gawk unfurled scrutiny

Discussion Questions

1. How do the three sisters compare to one another? What role does each play in the family? *(As the eldest, Delphine takes care of her sisters. She often puts her desires and fears aside so she can give her sisters what they want or need. On the airplane, Vonetta and Fern are afraid, so Delphine tries to ease their fears. She says, "That's mainly what I do. Keep Vonetta and Fern in line" [p. 2]. Delphine also shows her maturity when she gives up the window seat on the plane to prevent fighting between Vonetta and Fern, refuses money from a lady at the airport, accompanies her sisters through the airport while Cecile walks ahead, and resolves the sleeping arrangements at Cecile's house. Vonetta is the middle child and loves attention. Delphine calls her "showy" and knows Vonetta plans to charm their mother with her cuteness. Fern is the youngest. She mixes fantasy with reality and thinks literally, telling Cecile, "We need night-beds. We sleep at night" [p. 26] after Cecile shows them the daybed they will be sleeping on. She often mimics and agrees with Delphine, which indicates that she looks up to her sister.)*

2. What can you tell about the relationship between African Americans and Caucasians during this time period from the girls' trip to Oakland? Why is Delphine offended by the white woman who admires the girls at the airport? *(Answers will vary. Throughout their journey, Delphine is keenly aware that their behavior is being watched and judged by the white people they encounter. She is afraid they will make a "Negro spectacle" of themselves on the plane, and when she causes a commotion trying to see out the window she feels she "had managed to disgrace the entire Negro race, judging by the head shaking and* tsk-tsking *going on around [them]" [p. 11]. Delphine feels the white woman is being condescending when she comments on how adorable and well-behaved she and her sisters are, "like [they] were on display at the Bronx Zoo" [p. 15].)*

3. Describe Big Ma. Based on the author's descriptions of Cecile, do you think Big Ma and Cecile would've gotten along if Cecile hadn't left? *(Big Ma moved from Alabama to live with the family after Cecile left. She is old-fashioned and doesn't acknowledge change [e.g., She refuses to refer to the airport as "JFK," its new, official name.]. It seems that she does not want to challenge the current situation between white and black people. Big Ma emphasizes to Delphine the need to be on her best behavior around white people, and Delphine thinks Big Ma would have been glad that the lady at the airport wanted to give the girls money for being cute. Big Ma greatly resents Cecile and "hadn't considered forgiveness where Cecile was concerned" [p. 4]. Delphine says Cecile would not be welcome by Big Ma in Brooklyn and that is why Pa sent them to Oakland. Answers will vary. When Cecile is introduced, she is disguised well. She wears a scarf around her head, big black sunglasses, a big hat, and men's pants—"like a colored movie star" [p. 20]. Cecile is rude and unpleasant when the girls meet her. Because Big Ma is old-fashioned and teaches good manners, it seems that she and Cecile wouldn't get along even if Cecile had stayed.)*

4. What do Cecile's actions at the airport and in the taxi indicate about her feelings toward the children's visit? *(Answers will vary. Cecile does not appear eager to see the girls. Delphine notices that Cecile "moved, then moved back, maybe deciding whether to come to [them] or not" [p. 18]. When Cecile claims the girls she refers to them as "these" instead of saying she is their mother. She doesn't help them with their suitcases and walks ahead of them quickly through the airport. Cecile might put distance between herself and the girls because she does not want people to see her with them. She hurries the children into the taxi and smokes a cigarette in front of them without considering how it affects them. Her actions seem to indicate a total lack of interest in the girls.)*

5. Based on the Background Information provided in this guide and the description of the cab driver, how do you think Cecile is associated with him? *(Answers will vary. Delphine says the driver is wearing a black beret and calls her mother a name that sounds like "Zilla." Since Black Panthers are well-known in Oakland at this time period and black berets are part of their uniform, he may be a Black Panther. This might indicate Cecile is also a Black Panther or that she helps them somehow.)*

6. Delphine recounts how Big Ma would say their mother lived on the street or "in a hole in the wall" (p. 23) and slept on park benches. How did these expressions add to Delphine's feelings of abandonment by her mother? *(As a six-year-old, Delphine took her grandmother's words literally. She pictured her mother living on the street in the worst conditions while it rained or snowed. This made it more difficult for her to understand why her mother would prefer such a lifestyle to living with Delphine and her sisters.)*

7. As the girls prepare to sleep in their mother's house the first night, Delphine thinks, "Our mother was crazy" (p. 27). Why does Delphine believe this? *(Delphine is referring to Cecile's strange behavior and characteristics. Cecile mutters to herself, places pencils in her hair, and dresses "like a secret agent" [p. 18]. Delphine also makes judgments based on her mother's house. Because Cecile's house seems strange to Delphine and is different from the other houses in the neighborhood, Delphine concludes that their mother ran away because she was crazy.)*

Supplementary Activities

1. Writing: On page 14 of the novel, Delphine mentions alternative names for "mother" and what each implies. Have students identify different names for "father" and provide a short description of what each implies (e.g., Dad, Daddy, Pa, etc.).
2. Point of View: *One Crazy Summer* uses first-person point of view. Use the T-chart on page 31 of this guide to compare the advantages and disadvantages of first-person narration.
3. History: Research Cassius Clay. Why was he famous, and why did he change his name? Create a chart of historic figures you encounter while reading the novel, including researched information for each.

Mean Lady Ming–Glass of Water

Cecile sends the girls to order takeout at Ming's Chinese restaurant. They also make a collect call home to their father and Big Ma. Three Black Panthers visit Cecile. Fern stands up to Cecile, demanding a glass of water and to be called by her name instead of "little girl." When Cecile refuses to call her by name, Delphine confirms Big Ma's notion that their mother left because Pa wouldn't let her name Fern.

Vocabulary
chimed slumping lag suspiciously fugitive kindling porcelain

Discussion Questions

1. Where does Cecile send the girls for food? Why is this a problem for the girls? Why do you think Cecile doesn't cook for them? *(Cecile sends the girls to a nearby Chinese restaurant to order food. Cecile has Delphine use the money their father gave them for Disneyland to buy the food, and she tells Delphine to order shrimp lo mein, egg rolls, and a bottle of Pepsi. The girls are accustomed to eating Big Ma's home-cooked meals and know eating takeout is not good for them. Delphine objects to drinking Pepsi and tells her mother she will order fruit punch instead. Delphine is also taken aback that Cecile is making them walk by themselves at night in an unfamiliar neighborhood. Answers will vary. Some students might think Cecile doesn't know how to cook and doesn't care to learn. Some might think she is not used to caring for others since she is accustomed to living alone. Still other students might think she doesn't care what the girls eat because she doesn't want to be distracted from her work.)*

2. Why does Delphine begin to refer to Ming as "Mean Lady Ming"? What indicates that Ming is also caring? *(Ming does not greet the girls when they enter the restaurant. She says "No free egg rolls" and "wave[s] her hands like 'Shoo, stray cat'" [p. 36] at the girls. Delphine says, "She muttered...and looked mean and tired..." [p. 37]. When Ming says, "Everybody poor. Everybody hungry. I give free egg roll. Feel sorry" [p. 37], she is showing she has compassion for others.)*

3. Describe Cecile's actions on pages 40–41 of the novel. How is she portrayed through these descriptions? *(Answers will vary. Suggestions: "Cecile took over everything, dumping shrimp...tossing everyone a fork..." [p. 40]. "...she broke the sticks...rubbed them against each other like she was kindling twigs for a campfire...and shoved the noodles, shrimp, and sticks into her mouth" [p. 41]. Cecile's actions show the ruggedness of her character and her lack of manners, setting a bad example for her daughters. Cecile is not very graceful when serving the food and is bossy toward Delphine. Delphine says, "This was the most mothering we got.... [Vonetta and Fern] were expecting a mother" [p. 40].)*

4. Based on Cecile's conversation with the three Black Panthers, what do you think they want from her? *(Answers will vary. The Black Panthers are fighting for "the people" and expect Cecile to contribute. She is a writer and owns a printing press, and the girls overhear her saying that paper, ink, her printing press, and Cecile herself are not free. One of the men also says, "...those who have extreme abilities will have to carry extremely heavy loads" [p. 46]. This might indicate that the Panthers have a high regard for Cecile's writing talent.)*

5. Find three examples from the novel that illustrate Delphine's sense of responsibility. How would you compare Delphine's sense of responsibility with your own? *(Suggestions: "...I would have opened a can of beans and fried up some franks. I can bake a chicken and boil potatoes. I would have never let my long-gone daughters travel nearly three thousand miles without turning on the stove" [p. 31]. "It's the clock part that matters anyway. I can count on it to keep things running on schedule" [p. 49]. "Wish all I wanted, I couldn't leave Vonetta and Fern alone to sort out who'd sleep at what end of the daybed.... I stuck to the schedule" [p. 50]. Answers will vary.)*

6. Why does Delphine find it so difficult to politely ask her mother to get a glass of water for Fern? Have you ever had to be polite to someone with whom you were angry? How did it make you feel? *(Cecile angers Delphine, and when Cecile refuses to give Fern water, Delphine is forced to ask nicely. Delphine may lack respect for Cecile and feel she doesn't deserve to be treated nicely since Cecile hasn't shown them kindness since they arrived in Oakland. Answers will vary.)*
7. How is Fern portrayed during the scene in which she asks for a glass of water? *(Fern is tough and indignant. When Cecile repeatedly calls her "little girl" instead of by name, Fern responds each time by saying, "I'm not Little Girl. I'm Fern" [p. 52]. Fern stands with balled fists when her mother continues to call her "little girl" and then takes the glass of water. She drinks the entire glass of water without stopping, probably "to prove she could" and "to not stand near Cecile any longer than she had to" [p. 54].)*
8. What do you know about Cecile so far? What further information might you want to know about her? *(Suggestions: Cecile left the family just after Fern was born possibly because of a disagreement about Fern's name; she is known as "Inzilla" rather than Cecile; she writes poetry; she did not get along with Big Ma; she is not very maternal; she owns a printing press; she is sufficiently well-off; she is a strong woman; she dresses as if to disguise herself. Answers will vary. Students might want to know exactly why she left, how she makes a living, why she didn't like Fern's name, why she doesn't let the girls in her kitchen, or how she is connected to the Black Panthers.)*

Supplementary Activities

1. History: Add the following people to your chart of historical figures: Eldridge Cleaver, Huey Newton, H. Rap Brown. Write a brief description of each person's role in the 1960s Civil Rights Movement.
2. Culture/Symbolism: In Delphine's descriptions of people, she often points out if they have Afros. Research the symbolic meaning of Afros to members of the African-American community during that time period. Present your findings to the class.
3. Figurative Language: Create a chart of similes and metaphors you find in this section. Examples: **Similes**—"...behind us crept a rumbling against concrete, like a barrel rolling..." (p. 34); "rubbed them against each other like she was kindling twigs for a campfire" (p. 41); "with more talk about 'the people' thrown in...like Big Ma throwing a pinch of salt into the cake batter" (p. 46); **Metaphors**—kids playing: wiggle worms, frozen statues (p. 34); the girls: trained spies (p. 43); Fern as an infant: a loaf of bread (p. 52)

Inseparable–Everyone Knows the King of the Sea

Cecile sends Delphine, Vonetta, and Fern to the People's Center, a Black Panther organization, for breakfast and to get them out of the house for the day. While there, the girls encounter a "wild" young man named Kelvin, who ridicules Fern for carrying a white doll, and Vonetta tries to befriend three sisters. Sister Mukumbu, whom the girls like instantly, gives a lesson about the revolution involving a demonstration with a boy named Hirohito. The girls question Cecile about the name "Nzila," which causes Delphine to remember the painful day she discovered her name was not unique.

Vocabulary
buckle refrained sullenly declaration uttered baffled documenting superior mammal

Discussion Questions

1. What causes Delphine to further believe her mother is crazy? How does the reader know this? *(Cecile advises the girls to go unaccompanied to the People's Center to eat breakfast. Delphine believes Cecile is crazy because the People's Center is owned by Black Panthers—"militant strangers." Cecile also tells them to do whatever they want afterward and that it doesn't matter to her. The reader knows Delphine considers her mother crazy because Delphine thinks this many times. When Cecile gives Delphine a box to give to the Black Panthers and tells Delphine to deliver a message to them from her, Delphine says, "I just took the box and nodded, because that's how you treat crazy people" [p. 58].)*

2. What happens when Fern carries Miss Patty Cake around the People's Center? What does Kelvin refer to Miss Patty Cake as, and why? *(Fern attracts attention because Miss Patty Cake is a white baby doll. First, Cecile comments that Fern is too big to be so attached to a doll. Then, at the Center a young man named Kelvin teases her about the doll's color. He refers to the doll as "self-hatred." Answers will vary. Kelvin may believe Fern should only play with black dolls since she is African-American. He asks her, "Are your eyes blue like hers? Is your hair blond like hers? Is your skin white like hers" [p. 66]? He might be offended that Fern is unaware of what she's perpetuating by carrying the doll.)*

3. After witnessing the girls' encounter with Kelvin, why do you think the Black Panthers said, "...Those are Sister Inzilla's, all right" (p. 67)? Why is this ironic? *(Answers will vary. Based on the descriptions of Cecile up until this point, the reader can conclude that she is a tough woman who can survive on her own and defend herself. When Fern stands up to Kelvin, preferring to be called "colored" instead of "black" and refusing to feel ashamed about her doll, she is showing she is unafraid to be herself. Delphine also channels Cecile when she defends Fern and tells the children to stop calling Fern names. It's ironic because the girls do not like their mother and feel they are nothing like her, yet they all have her attitude and sense of independence.)*

4. How does Vonetta differ from Delphine and Fern, and how is this apparent at the People's Center? *(Answers will vary. Of the three girls, Vonetta is the most social. She loves attention and making friends. When they arrive at the Center, Delphine says, "Vonetta was already smiling and showing anyone who'd look her way that she was worth a smile back" [p. 62]. When Vonetta sees the three sisters in fashionable dresses and go-go boots, she immediately tries to befriend them, while Delphine is not interested. Vonetta seems to need more approval from others than either Fern or Delphine. When Fern is being ridiculed for carrying Miss Patty Cake, "Vonetta ate her toast silently" [p. 67], leaving Delphine to defend Fern. Vonetta's desire for attention becomes apparent when she impulsively speaks out in class, saying, "We didn't come for the revolution. We came for breakfast" [p. 73]. Her desire to impress seems to make her less independent than her sisters, who don't seem to care as much about what others think.)*

5. What does Delphine mean when she describes herself and her father as "plain"? How might Cecile and Pa's differences have affected Cecile's decision to leave? *(Answers will vary. Delphine highlights a major difference between her parents. Cecile is a poet who often fantasizes and wants to use her poetry to change the world. Delphine and her father are more concerned about the daily practicalities of living. Delphine says, "I didn't know about blowing dust and clearing paths. I knew about hot-combing thick heads of hair and ironing...skirts for school" [p. 76]. Cecile might have felt smothered by Pa's household, unable to express herself. Because Pa is more sensible and not as artistic as Cecile, he wanted a familiar name for Fern, telling Cecile, "No more of those made-up, different names" [p. 81]. Cecile wanted to be free to express herself creatively, but Pa often stifled Cecile's ability to do so. Cecile was ultimately ill-equipped to handle these differences and chose instead to leave her family.)*
6. Explain why Delphine was so upset to discover her name in the dictionary. Do you agree with the importance Delphine places on names? *(Delphine believes "Your name is who you are and how you're known even when you do something great or something dumb" [p. 80]. She loves the idea of her name being unique and something she doesn't have to share with anyone else. Since Vonetta's name was inspired by the singer Sarah Vaughan, and naming Fern what Cecile "dreamed up" was so important, Delphine assumed her name had such meaning, also. When Delphine found her name in the dictionary she thought, "This changed everything. My mother hadn't reached into her poetic soul and dreamt me up a name. My mother had given me a name that already was, which meant she hadn't given me a thing" [p. 84]. Answers will vary. Some students might believe Delphine's disappointment is understandable since she feels her name is the only thing her mother ever gave her. Other students might believe Delphine places too much importance on names and that she shouldn't be so upset.)*

Supplementary Activities

1. Map/Drawing: Study Cecile's directions to the People's Center. Then, draw a map showing the girls' route to the Center, marking the beginning and end points.
2. Poetry: Adopt a poet's name for your own, as Cecile did, and write a poem about the people or events happening in the area you live.
3. History/Speaking: Research COINTELPRO and the program's purpose. Who instituted this program, and what were some of the tactics they used to infiltrate the Black Panthers? Discuss with your classmates whether you believe these tactics were ethical or not, and why.
4. Writing: Research the meaning of your name online or in a baby name book. Write a paragraph discussing the origin of your name and how you feel about it.

Coloring and La-La–Big Red *S*

Vonetta does not defend Fern when one of the Ankton sisters makes fun of Fern. Later, Vonetta colors Miss Patty Cake black with a marker. Delphine cannot scrub the marker off the doll and must keep Fern and Vonetta separated. Delphine and Fern sort the Black Panther weekly newspapers at the Center, and Delphine becomes interested in the stories. When Fern gets an upset stomach, Delphine decides to ignore Cecile's rule about staying out of the kitchen and makes a home-cooked meal.

Vocabulary

indulgence
begrudgingly
amiss
defiant
prospect
accountable
knack
tempted
hovered
blanched
yokes

Discussion Questions

1. Why does Delphine feel relieved as she watches the interaction between the white men delivering bread and the Black Panthers? After "Crazy Kelvin" makes a hateful comment about the men, what does Delphine mean when she says, "...he spoiled what I thought I knew" (p. 87)? *(Delphine feels at ease because she sees them talking and laughing. She thought they would fight or something bad would happen. When Delphine sees that the men are being friendly with each other, she begins to realize that not all the Panthers are the violent "militants" portrayed on television. She says Kelvin "spoiled what [she] thought [she] knew" [p. 87] because as she begins to think "This place is all right" [p. 87], he calls the white men "racist dogs" after they leave.)*
2. What is your impression of Kelvin at this point? How is he different from Sister Mukumbu and Sister Pat? *(Answers will vary. Students might mention how Kelvin is more outspoken and aggressive and enjoys bullying people, whereas Sister Mukumbu and Sister Pat are caring and accepting of others. They teach and feed the people who attend the Center.)*
3. Why doesn't Vonetta defend Fern when the Ankton girl teases her? What do you think of Vonetta's decision? *(Vonetta enjoys making friends and being social. She deeply cares about her outward appearance, and since she's been trying to befriend the Ankton sisters for some time, she wants to make a good impression. Answers will vary.)*
4. Why does Vonetta color Miss Patty Cake black? How does this affect the sisters' relationship? *(Answers will vary. As Delphine mentions earlier, she and Vonetta have often had to defend Fern and her doll to other people. Vonetta might have been tired of defending Fern and maybe even losing friends over it. Vonetta might have been so embarrassed and upset that she wanted to ruin the doll so Fern wouldn't carry it around anymore and she wouldn't have to worry about anyone making fun of Fern. Vonetta might also have colored the doll black just to be cruel and prove a point. The sisters become divided after Vonetta colors Miss Patty Cake. Fern becomes very sad, and Delphine keeps Vonetta and Fern separated for the rest of the night. Instead of Fern showering and sleeping with Vonetta, she sleeps with Delphine. The next day, Vonetta doesn't show any remorse for her action. Delphine says she "remained proudly defiant, walking two steps ahead of us and then leaving us altogether once her new friends, the Anktons, were in sight" [p. 97].)*
5. Why is it significant that Delphine uses the dimes she and her sisters are saving to buy a newspaper? *(Answers will vary. By spending the dimes on the paper instead of keeping them to call home, Delphine shows she is becoming more interested and involved in a world that initially seemed foreign and unwelcoming to her. When she arrived in Oakland, she greatly disliked the city and wanted to leave. She did not want to go to the People's Center the first time Cecile sent them there, but now she enjoys participating in the activities and meals.)*

6. What does Cecile mean when she says, "We're trying to break yokes. You're trying to make one for yourself. If you knew what I know, seen what I've seen, you wouldn't be so quick to pull the plow" (p. 110)? What major difference between Cecile and Delphine is shown during their encounter after Delphine's home-cooked dinner? *(The metaphor illustrates the role minority groups have long played in America. As a tough black woman, Cecile doesn't want to be in service to anyone, including her children. She tells Delphine to be more selfish, but Delphine, like her father, is more practical. Delphine doesn't care if she must cook meals for her sisters and clean up afterward because she knows it needs to be done. Students could discuss the contradiction of Cecile devouring the meal and then berating Delphine for cooking it.)*
7. Do you think Delphine takes on too much responsibility? Why or why not? *(Answers will vary. Some students might think Delphine has to take responsibility for her sisters since her mother isn't there for them. Other students might think she should just be a kid and enjoy her childhood.)*

Supplementary Activities

1. History: Add "Li'l Bobby" to your chart of historical figures. What was his real name, and why do the Black Panthers remember him?
2. Creative Writing: Using the voice of Delphine, Vonetta, or Fern, write a letter to Big Ma or Pa about your visit in Oakland so far.
3. Research: Research other resistance movement publications (e.g., *Anti-Slavery Examiner* and the leaflets produced by the anti-Nazi group White Rose). Then, write a brief report about your findings.
4. Poetry: Write an acrostic poem using the word "revolution."

China Who–Eating Crow

The girls ask Cecile for a television but receive an old radio instead. Delphine learns that Hirohito is both African-American and Japanese and that his father was put in prison "because he dared speak the truth to the people" (p. 123). Delphine becomes uneasy about participating in the Black Panthers' activities after she finds out about Hirohito's father and the shooting of Bobby Hutton. Sister Mukumbu announces that everyone from the Center will be attending a rally honoring Huey and Bobby Hutton. Delphine decides attending would be too dangerous and says she and her sisters will not participate, but Cecile makes them anyway.

Vocabulary
complexion ignorance incident flummoxed civics rally lure vain gesturing reeling calisthenics cackling

Discussion Questions

1. Discuss why it is ironic that Delphine calls Cecile "the Establishment" when she is determining how to ask Cecile for a television. Note: Explain the term "Anti-Establishment" and how it was used in the 1960s, the era of youth protests. *(Delphine sees Cecile as "the Establishment" because "the Establishment was someone over thirty years old who had the power" [p. 117], and Delphine assumes Cecile is over 30. This is ironic because Cecile is involved in a struggle against the established rules and order of society.)*
2. What is "colored counting," and what are some of the results the girls have gotten from doing this? Why do the girls "color count"? *(The girls call it "colored counting" when they count the number of black people on TV shows and commercials. They also count the number of words the actors are given. The girls have found that the number of words the actors speak range from none at all to too many to count. They also notice that black people are often in commercials for deodorant, shaving cream, wash powder, and butter. Delphine says that the little girl from the butter commercial had a "dead, expressionless voice.... Not too colored" [p. 119]. Answers will vary. The girls may play this game because they want to prove how underrepresented African Americans are on television and show the kinds of roles they are cast in. Some students may think the girls play the game for fun since Delphine does not seem upset in her narration. She seems to joke about it rather than complain.)*
3. When Kelvin is harassing Hirohito about his father, what does Delphine mean when she says, "Hirohito tried to show no change in his face, but he was changing on the inside, where people change when they're sad or angry" (p. 123)? Do you think Delphine is speaking from personal experience? *(Answers will vary. Delphine is saying that although Hirohito is trying not to show his emotions on the outside, he is still being affected by the topic Kelvin is talking so openly about. Students might think Delphine knows this from personal experience, since it seems that she understands exactly how he is feeling.)*
4. Recalling the girls' trip to Alabama with their father, Delphine says she is surprised he didn't tell Big Ma about what happened on the drive there. Why do you think Pa didn't tell Big Ma about the policeman? *(Answers will vary. Pa might have been humiliated and wanted to forget about it, or he might have believed there was no reason to tell Big Ma. Pa might have also been used to that kind of treatment in that part of the country.)*

5. Why does Delphine become upset after learning about Bobby Hutton's death? *(Delphine finds out Bobby was only six years older than she is when he was killed and that he was "the youngest Black Panther to die for the cause" [pp. 126–127]. This upsets her because she feels he was too young to die and that if he wouldn't have been involved with the Panthers he would still be alive. When she looks around at everyone at the Center, she feels afraid that they could end up like Bobby. Delphine especially becomes afraid for her sisters.)*
6. Why doesn't Sister Mukumbu or Cecile believe the rally will be dangerous? Do you think Delphine is right to want to keep her sisters away? *(Answers will vary. Sister Mukumbu might be a little concerned about the rally, but she seems to believe the purpose of the rally is more important. She reminds Delphine that "The rally is one way of looking out for all of our sisters. All of our brothers.... We have to stand united" [p. 133]. Cecile seems indifferent about the rally. Her main concern seems to be to get the girls out of the house.)*
7. What does "eating crow" mean? What does Delphine have to "eat crow" about? What causes her to reconsider her opinion of Eunice? *("Eating crow" is a metaphor for swallowing your pride about an issue. Delphine says it's like "swallowing a hunk of tough, chewy crow meat that wasn't about to go down easy" [p. 137]. She has to "eat crow" about attending the rally and becoming friends with Eunice Ankton. Delphine and Eunice bond over their position as the oldest sister of three. They also both believe their younger sisters [Vonetta and Janice] are foolish for chasing Hirohito. Delphine decides she likes Eunice when she finds out Eunice's mother hand-stitched her nice dress. Delphine realizes Eunice doesn't think she's better than Delphine. Delphine says, "We were two older sisters watching our younger sisters.... We were both the oldest girls in our families, and we knew the same things" [p. 139].)*

Supplementary Activities

1. Figurative Language/Art: Delphine often uses idiomatic expressions, such as "eating crow" and "spinning straw" when she speaks. Look at the following list of expressions. Illustrate at least five of them, and explain how you think each originated.

   Don't put all your eggs in one basket.

   Every cloud has a silver lining.

   A bird in the hand is worth two in the bush.

   A rolling stone gathers no moss.

   The early bird gets the worm.

   A fool and his money are soon parted.

   A stitch in time saves nine.

   The squeaky wheel gets the grease.

   Fish and visitors smell in three days.

   You made your bed, now lie in it.

2. Reading Journal: Write a journal entry explaining your ideas about the girls' game of "colored counting" when they watch television. Write why you think they do this and how it might make them feel.

Itsy Bitsy Spider–Wish We Had a Camera

Vonetta practices the Gwendolyn Brooks poem she is going to recite for the rally. Cecile gets Delphine a stool to sit on while Delphine cooks dinner. Cecile also teaches Delphine how to use her printing machine and tells Delphine to try printing one of her poems, but is immediately critical of Delphine's first attempt. The girls take a bus to San Francisco to go sightseeing. While on the bus, Fern sees something but gleefully refuses to tell her sisters what she saw. After an exciting day of sightseeing, the girls come home to find police cars outside Cecile's house and Cecile being led away in handcuffs.

Vocabulary
shiftless perfectionist recitation needle excursion uncomprehending rambling agog majestic stewing

Discussion Questions

1. Why does Delphine say Vonetta is just like Cecile? Do you agree? Why or why not? *(Delphine says Vonetta is just like Cecile because Vonetta places her own interests and desires above everyone else's. Cecile keeps to herself and cares only for her writing, even when the girls visit and need Cecile's attention. Delphine proves this to Vonetta when she poses a hypothetical situation of Vonetta supporting her own child or pursuing her own, more glamorous, interests. Answers will vary.)*

2. What evidence shows that Cecile is starting to acknowledge the girls more? *(Answers will vary. In the previous section, instead of completely ignoring the girls' request for a TV, Cecile gives them a radio. Then, Delphine finds Cecile has brought a stool into the kitchen for Delphine to sit on while she cooks. She must have noticed Delphine's aching feet, even though it was never apparent she was looking. Cecile shares her poetry with Delphine, teaching her about the printer and inviting her to print a poem. It's the first time Cecile has volunteered any direct contact. She also indirectly supports the girls' outing to San Francisco by freely giving them the money they need for the trip.)*

3. Do you think Delphine is being honest about her feelings for Hirohito? What clues are given that show she might like him as more than a friend? *(Answers will vary. Although Delphine pretends to dislike Hirohito, the reader might question her true feelings, as she continually tries to show her disregard for him. When the sisters encounter Hirohito on the way to the bus stop, Delphine says, "I couldn't say it was thrilling, how he jumped on that board thing and rolled down the hill.... I couldn't say how I admired him for not crying about his father being in prison and for trying to be a normal kid..." [p. 156]. When she says this, she is showing that she does find him interesting but doesn't want to show it. Then, while on the bus, she keeps thinking about him and realizes he said,* "Delphine. Want to watch me fly down that hill" *[p. 158]? She is pleased that he directed the question to her and not Vonetta or Fern.)*

4. Delphine says, "I can study every move Fern makes and still not completely know her. There are just things I don't understand about her the way I understand Vonetta" (p. 157). Why do you think it's more difficult for Delphine to understand Fern than Vonetta? *(Answers will vary. Throughout the story, Delphine describes Vonetta as a show-off who craves attention. Delphine is aware of and understands Vonetta's motives. It may be more difficult for Delphine to understand Fern because Fern is still young and hasn't yet adopted a defining quality. Delphine finds that Fern is unpredictable, especially when she copes surprisingly well with the loss of her beloved doll.)*

5. During the girls' trip to San Francisco, what instances show that the Black Panthers have had an influence on them? *(When the hippies greet the girls at the bus stop in San Francisco with "Peace," the girls respond with "Power to the people" and "Free Huey" [p. 160]. When they are shopping for souvenirs at Fisherman's Wharf and are treated rudely by the clerk who suspects they will shoplift, Delphine tells him, "We are citizens, and we demand respect" [p. 164]. Delphine realizes afterward that Big Ma would have wanted her to be respectful and say "'Yes, sir' and 'Please, sir' to show him [they] were just as civilized as everyone else" [p. 165]. Delphine comments, "I had that Black Panther stuff in me, and it was pouring out at every turn" [p. 164].)*
6. Why do you think the police arrest Cecile? *(Answers will vary. Students might refer to the fact that Hirohito's father was arrested for speaking "the truth" to the people. Students might also consider that Cecile aides the Black Panthers in "the cause" and it seems that anyone involved with the Panthers is viewed as dangerous by the police.)*

Supplementary Activities

1. Poetry: Read and discuss Gwendolyn Brooks's poem titled "We Real Cool." Then, listen to a recording of Brooks reading the poem at http://www.poets.org/viewmedia.php/prmMID/15433 (active at time of publication).
2. Art/Creative Thinking: Throughout the girls' trip to San Francisco, Delphine often says she wished they had a camera to keep the memories of all they see. Create a scrapbook of the girls' trip using your choice of medium for images (e.g., drawings, paintings, copyright-free downloads from the Internet, personal photos).
3. Journal: Write a journal entry telling about a place you would like to visit. Tell why you want to go there and what you would expect to do and see there.

The Clark Sisters–Glorious Hill

Cecile tells the police she does not have kids in order to save Delphine, Vonetta, and Fern from possible separation. After the police leave, the girls enter the house and discover the kitchen has been torn up and Cecile's movable type sets have been scattered around the room. The next day, while the girls are cleaning the house, they find a poem by Cecile called "I Birthed a Nation" and realize it's about them. Hirohito and his mother bring dinner and invite the girls to stay with them until Cecile returns. Delphine, Vonetta, and Fern help distribute flyers around town in support of the rally. Hirohito convinces Delphine to ride his go-kart, and she finally allows herself to have fun.

Vocabulary
clumsy empowered respectful snickered swiveled glorious

Discussion Questions

1. How is Cecile's denial of her children beneficial for them and different than how she usually treats them? *(Cecile only denies the girls because she is trying to protect them. She doesn't want the police to take them into custody and potentially split them up. By saying they belong to someone else, she keeps them out of the authorities' hands. This time she's not acting out of selfishness or disinterest, as is usually the case regarding the girls.)*
2. Why do the girls take so much time and care to restore Cecile's kitchen to order? *(Answers will vary. It might be because the parent-child bond is not easily broken. Despite Cecile's neglect, she remains the girls' mother, and therefore, they still care and want to help; they may feel it is the right thing to do. The girls might take a certain amount of pride in their mother being a poet, as Delphine earlier recalled telling her class about Cecile. The girls might understand how important Cecile's work and kitchen are to her, and they want to please her by repairing the damage.)*
3. What does Mrs. Woods mean when she tells the girls, "We know the same things. We have to stick together" (p. 178)? *(Mrs. Woods is referring to her experience of Hirohito's father being taken away by the police. She understands what the girls are going through and wants to support them. Mrs. Woods is putting the girls at ease by assuring them she will take care of them. Mrs. Woods and the girls both live with the uncertainty of when their loved ones will return.)*
4. Sister Mukumbu tells the children, "Information is power..." (p. 181). What does this mean? Give some examples from the novel and from real life to support your response. *(Answers will vary. Sister Mukumbu is referring to Cecile volunteering her printing services to the Black Panthers to help spread information to the people. Sister Mukumbu says, "Keeping the people informed keeps the people empowered" [p. 181]. Since the girls have started attending the Center, they have learned much about their basic rights and now notice when they are being treated unjustly so they can defend themselves. The girls display their understanding of this lesson when they stand up to the man who assumes they will steal from his souvenir shop. This lesson in civil rights would have been beneficial to Pa when he was pulled over and treated unjustly by a policeman on the drive to Alabama. The reader might also believe that if Hirohito's father knew his rights he could have defended himself against the police who burst into his home. Encourage students to provide several real-life examples.)*
5. Why might store owners be "no sayers" who refuse to hang flyers in their stores for the rally? Do you think Delphine's decision to never shop at Safeway again will make a difference? *(Answers will vary. Stores might refuse the flyers because they do not care and therefore do not want to support the cause. Delphine says, "The hardened looks of grown-ups who didn't like kids or black people, or kids who were black, were nothing new to us" [p. 183]. If the store owners are racist against African Americans, then they might refuse the flyers to keep people uninformed. Other stores,*

such as Safeway, may be reluctant to get involved out of fear or policy. Some students might think Delphine's decision won't affect Safeway because she is only one person, but the manager might notice she is standing up for what she believes in. Other students might think she could affect his business in a negative way, however, if she convinced others to no longer shop there.)

6. What changes in Delphine are noticeable in the chapter "Glorious Hill"? *(For the first time, Delphine is able to act like a carefree kid instead of the responsible person she must usually be. Although reluctant at first, Delphine learns how it feels to relax and not have to do chores all day since Mrs. Woods will not allow her to work. Hirohito convinces her to take a ride on his go-kart down the hill. When she finally rides down the hill she says, "I had never heard myself scream.... Screamed and hiccupped and laughed like my sisters. Like I was having the time of my life, flying down that glorious hill" [pp. 190–191]. Her narration shows that she is truly having fun for the first time.)*

Supplementary Activities

1. Writing: Write a paragraph describing something you love to do. What makes it enjoyable for you? Is this activity something adults would enjoy? Why or why not?
2. Figurative Language: Ask the teacher to place pictures of different items (e.g., pencil, spoon, flower, paperclip, comb, etc.) in a bag. Without looking, select a picture from the bag, and complete the following analogy.

   ____________________ is like a(n) ________________________ because
   (character from novel) (item name)

   ____

   ____.

The Third Thing–Afua

The day of the rally arrives, and Delphine is proud as she sees over 1,000 people in attendance. The girls recite their mother's poem, "I Birthed a Nation," adding the word "black" throughout. Fern recites her own poem about Crazy Kelvin. The girls are happy to discover Cecile was in the audience for their recitation, as they seek further signs of approval from her. Delphine and Hirohito admit their feelings for each other. Cecile criticizes Delphine for not calling Pa while Cecile was in jail, and Delphine becomes angry and yells back at her. Cecile talks to Delphine about her past and the moment she left them. Delphine tells Fern her real name is Afua. The girls return to the airport to travel back to California and give their mother a hug goodbye.

Vocabulary

perched
patrolling
dramatic
ashen
atone
consoled
braced
gushing

Discussion Questions

1. What is Cecile's poem "I Birthed a Nation" about? Why do you think Vonetta decided to add the word "black" in several places? Do you think it changes the poem's effectiveness or meaning? *(The poem is about "Mother Africa" lamenting the loss of her children to slavery and oppression oceans away. She is sad for the loss of her children, the suffering of the enslaved, and the ongoing separation. Answers will vary. Vonetta might have added the word "black" to show she is proud to be African American. It also indicates that the girls have accepted the term, since when they came to Oakland they preferred to be called "colored" rather than "black.")*
2. What is Fern saying through her poem about Crazy Kelvin? What made Fern keep "Crazy Kelvin in her sights" (p. 199)? *(Fern is explaining what she saw while on the bus to San Francisco. Her poem is telling everyone that Kelvin is an informant for the police. Delphine says that if Kelvin hadn't attracted so much attention trying to show his dislike for the "racist pigs," Fern probably wouldn't have thought anything of Kelvin's friendly encounter with the policeman. Delphine says that Fern might have watched Kelvin closely because of how he teased Fern about Miss Patty Cake, "telling her who she could love...who she was" [p. 199].)*
3. How is Cecile different after her stay in jail? What do you think has brought about the changes in her? *(Cecile comes back less guarded and less angry. Delphine says, "...Cecile just seemed different after having been locked up" [p. 200]. Cecile does not get mad at the girls for changing her poem, limits her disguise to big sunglasses, and compliments the girls. Cecile also publicly and proudly claims her daughters, saying to the organizers, "Y'all heard my daughters.... They said it all for me" [p. 201]. Answers will vary. Cecile might just be happy to be out of jail, or she might genuinely be proud of her girls. Cecile might feel more connected to them after hearing them recite her poem and Fern recite her own poem.)*
4. How do you view Cecile and her actions toward the girls after learning about her past? Do you think knowing a person's past is important in order to understand them? *(Answers will vary. Some students might be able to understand Cecile more and justify her actions. Some students might feel sympathy for her but still believe she shouldn't have abandoned her children.)*
5. What are the different emotions Delphine experiences during the conversation with her mother after the rally? What is the purpose of this conversation? *(At first, Delphine is disappointed because she receives no praise from Cecile for restoring the kitchen and taking care of her sisters. Delphine is enraged, "spilling-over mad" because instead of gratitude from Cecile she receives judgment. Delphine also experiences sadness and more anger when her mother talks about the past. Delphine says, "...all I could think about was my own self. What I lost. What I missed" [p. 209]. Then, Delphine becomes overwhelmed by all the information. Answers will vary.*

Through the conversation, Delphine learns about her mother's past: the death of Cecile's mother, Cecile's life on the street, the origins of her love of poetry, how she met Pa. Cecile might have told Delphine about her life so Delphine can understand the hardships she endured. Cecile might want Delphine to know that she should release some of her responsibilities and "Be eleven while [she] can" [p. 210]. Cecile might think Delphine is taking on unnecessary hardships.)

6. What did Cecile want to name Fern? Based on Delphine's belief about names, why might Cecile have refused to call Fern by her name? *(Cecile wanted to name Fern Afua. It is an African name, unique like Delphine's and Vonetta's. Answers will vary. Delphine realizes it doesn't matter what their names are, but that they got them from Cecile. This might be the reason Cecile refused to use Fern's name. Cecile might have felt it would be the only thing she could give to Fern, and not being able to caused her to feel less connected to Fern.)*
7. Compare and contrast the airport scene at the beginning of the story with the one at the end. What changes in Cecile and the girls are apparent? *(Answers will vary. Cecile stops the man at the airport from taking the girls' picture. This situation is similar to the woman who tries to give the girls money at the beginning, except Cecile isn't there to stop them from taking it and Delphine must. This time Cecile protects them, telling the man they are not "monkeys on display" [p. 214]. Delphine says, "I felt bad for him, but I knew Cecile had to step in. Any mother would have at least done that" [p. 214]. In the beginning, Cecile arrives late to pick up the girls and barely notices them. There are no hugs or warm greetings. Delphine expects the same at their goodbye but finds that Cecile is looking at her as the girls get in the line: "It was a strange, wonderful feeling. To discover eyes upon you when you expected no one to notice you at all" [p. 214]. Lastly, the girls hug Cecile for the first time.)*

Supplementary Activities

1. Creative Writing: Rewrite the final airport scene from Cecile's point of view.
2. Speaking: Discuss how each of the following elements of the setting contributes to the novel and the themes it explores.
    a. 1968
    b. Oakland, California
    c. Cecile's green stucco house
    d. the People's Center

Post-reading Discussion Questions

1. Even though the Gaither girls did not grow up with their mother, they exhibit some of her qualities. Tell which qualities each of the girls shares with Cecile. *(Fern shares her mother's poetic nature. Through the incident with Kelvin, Fern illustrates the ability to keenly observe people and situations. In a letter that Cecile later writes to Delphine, she tells her that on the day of the rally "a poet had been born" [p. 199]. Like Cecile, Fern is tough and gets angry when people mistreat her. Her trademark sign of frustration is balled fists by her side. Vonetta shares Cecile's self-centeredness. Delphine uses a hypothetical situation to prove that Vonetta is just like Cecile. In this situation, Vonetta chooses to miss her daughter's performance at school so she can perform on TV. Like Cecile, Vonetta does not see herself giving up her dreams in the interest of her children. Delphine shares Cecile's intelligence and strength. As a poet, Cecile often thinks about events taking place in the world. She seems to be a smart, insightful person. Delphine's intelligence is evident throughout the story, since she is constantly taking care of Vonetta and Fern and making decisions in their best interest. Given Cecile's past, she has learned to be strong and provide for herself. This same trait is seen in Delphine, since she not only takes care of her sisters' physical needs but also defends them when needed.)*

2. Compare Big Ma's view of how a black woman should behave to Cecile's. Which of these views has the most influence on the girls? *(Big Ma's approach is to get along and be peaceful. She makes sure that the girls are polite and well-behaved around white people to make a good impression. Delphine keeps this in mind as she navigates the Oakland airport with her sisters: "I did as Big Ma had told me in our many talks on how to act around white people" [p. 16]. When Delphine declines the money from the white woman, she does so in a tone "polite enough to suit Big Ma but strong enough to suit Papa" [p. 16]. Cecile has an opposite view and believes that Big Ma is old-fashioned and a relic of old Southern black attitudes. Once, when Delphine says "Yes, ma'am" to her mother, Cecile replies, "That's the problem right there. His mammy. You sound just like her. Like a country mule" [p. 136]. Cecile is not concerned with making a good impression or getting along. She asserts herself as an individual, making her own way—thus the poet name she chooses, Nzila, meaning "the path." At the beginning of the story, Big Ma's influence on the girls is most evident. Delphine constantly watches her sisters' and her own behavior, making sure it meets Big Ma's expectations. But after some time in Oakland, they begin to be more assertive. These contrasting attitudes surface in the gift shop in San Francisco. Delphine decides to defend herself and her sisters and walk out of the store, but as she does she thinks, "But I was sure Big Ma would have wanted us to say 'Yes, sir' and 'Please, sir' to show him we were just as civilized as everyone else" [p. 165].)*

3. Recall the many places in the story where the idea of names comes up. What does the author try to convey about the meaning and importance of names? *(Cecile renames herself Nzila. Delphine recalls the time when she was upset to learn that her name isn't original. Cecile ultimately leaves when she is unable to name Fern [although there is more to Cecile's decision]. It is very important to Fern that Cecile calls her by name. Answers will vary. Williams-Garcia is exploring the importance of names to a person's identity. To Cecile, a unique name becomes symbolic of a person, which is a belief Delphine shares, as seen in her disappointment at finding her name in the dictionary. It's often considered disrespectful not to acknowledge a person by name. People speak in terms of "guarding their good name," which is another indication of how our names and our dignity are connected. This is why Fern gets so frustrated that her mother calls her "Little Girl" instead of Fern. When Cecile doesn't use her name, Fern feels as if she doesn't matter to her mother. Another example is when the policeman in Alabama refused to call Pa by name, which was greatly disrespectful toward Pa.)*

4. Although the girls and Cecile are not very happy about the visit at the beginning of the story, how do you think they feel at the end? Be sure to support your response with specific details from the story. *(Answers will vary. After the girls return from their outing to San Francisco, it is clear that they feel much more comfortable with their surroundings. Delphine says, "...I was glad to be back in black Oakland..." [p. 166]. The girls establish new friendships with the Ankton girls and Hirohito. Sister Mukumbu and Sister Pat also become fond of the girls and hope they will return the next summer. As the time for departure approaches, Delphine reports that she felt "queasiness churning inside" [p. 214]. Although Cecile doesn't show her happiness and comfort with the girls as obviously, some students might believe she is happy with the girls' visit. Cecile puts a stool in the kitchen for Delphine, gives the girls a radio, compliments them after their poetry recitation, and finally uses Fern's name. Other examples include Cecile telling Delphine to help her print a poem, explaining her past to Delphine, waiting for the girls to board the plane, and accepting the girls' hugs. Delphine also mentions that Cecile wrote her a letter a month later, indicating that she stays in contact with her daughters.)*

5. Explain how each of the following objects becomes a symbol of the character to whom it belongs: Delphine's Timex, Cecile's printing press, Fern's doll, and Hirohito's go-kart. *(Answers will vary. The Timex becomes a symbol of Delphine's sense of responsibility. When she first mentions the watch she says, "...I was the only one responsible enough to keep and wear a wristwatch" [p. 8]. Delphine carefully times her sisters' baths and is very meticulous when planning the trip to San Francisco. It's significant that in the end, when she is learning to relax a little, she says, "I stopped glancing up at the big clock or down at my Timex" [p. 214]. The printing press embodies Cecile's love of the written word. It also shows her sense of independence, because with her own press she is truly in control of distributing her works. Miss Patty Cake has been Fern's close companion since the day she was born. The doll was actually the last thing Cecile gave to her the day she left. The doll gives Fern something to love when her mother is gone. This is why Delphine is puzzled by Fern's acceptance of the loss of Miss Patty Cake. Perhaps now that Fern is with her mother, she doesn't need the doll. Hirohito's go-kart is symbolic of his father. Hirohito tells Delphine that his father made the go-kart, and in the absence of his father, it becomes his stable companion.)*

6. How does each of the girls change during the four weeks in Oakland? *(Answers will vary. Vonetta seems to become more confident and mature by the end of the story. She takes the microphone at the rally with confidence and initiates the change to Cecile's poem. Her addition of the word "black" indicates that perhaps she has a different understanding of what it means to be a young black woman. Fern also shows maturity when she quickly accepts her loss of Miss Patty Cake and moves on. She is courageous when she recites her own poem at the rally, revealing who Kelvin is. Delphine learns to be a kid and have fun, like when she rides down the hill on Hirohito's go-kart. She also becomes less worried about everything her sisters do and does not intervene when they tease each other. Delphine also acknowledges her needs for the first time. She finally complains to her mother about all the responsibility she has accepted because Cecile wasn't there for them.)*

7. How has the girls' understanding of the world changed after their month in Oakland? *(Answers will vary. Under Big Ma's influence, the girls had learned to make a good impression on white people and to be polite no matter what. The girls also believed that all Black Panthers were dangerous and should be feared because that is how the Panthers were portrayed on TV. After spending time at the Center with Sister Mukumbu and Sister Pat, they realize not all of the Panthers are dangerous. The girls witness the good work that Sister Mukumbu and Sister Pat do for the community. The girls' world is opened up to the true meaning of revolution. They experience what it's like to be directly involved in a cause that can make history and change the world.)*

8. How would you describe Delphine's relationship with her sisters? How is your relationship with your siblings (or close friends or relatives) similar to or different from Delphine's? Would you want Delphine as a big sister? Why or why not? *(Answers will vary. Delphine acts as a mother to her sisters and takes responsibility for them. She makes all the decisions in her sisters' best interest because she is the oldest. Fern and Vonetta seem to accept her authority and rely on her. The only time they don't listen to Delphine is when Cecile contradicts her and tells the girls to go to the rally. Delphine and Vonetta don't always get along because they have clashing personalities. Vonetta loves attention and making good impressions on people, and sometimes this annoys Delphine. Delphine and Fern share a special bond. Since Fern is the youngest, Delphine feels she needs to protect her more, and Delphine always sides with Fern against Vonetta. Delphine and Fern's special bond is strengthened by the fact that Delphine was present at Fern's birth and practically raised her. Delphine may also feel more connected because Fern listens to her and looks up to her. Delphine may hope Fern will be more like her instead of Vonetta. Despite their differences, it seems the girls share a special closeness. Delphine says, "Following each other was easy. We'd been doing it for as long as we could all talk" [p. 197]. Students might mention Delphine's sense of responsibility, care, love, and intelligence when discussing if they'd want her as an older sister. Other students might feel she is too bossy and wouldn't want their sister telling them what to do.)*

9. How do the girls adapt to their new environment in Oakland? *(The girls are accustomed to Big Ma and her rules, so when they arrive in Oakland everything changes for them. They are forced to walk outside by themselves at night, they eat takeout for dinner and on the floor instead of at a table, and they are given much more freedom. They are used to Big Ma's caring and protective nature and thus are uncomfortable with Cecile ordering them out of the house every day. But the girls adapt quickly to these changes and begin to enjoy their stay. They end up liking the Center and the people there. They accept Cecile and her strangeness, and they quickly settle into the routine of Cecile's life. The only change Delphine refuses to accept is eating take-out food every day. Because she is responsible and knows her sisters need better food, she buys groceries and forces Cecile to allow her to use the kitchen.)*

10. How will the girls' relationship with Cecile and Big Ma change and/or progress? *(Answers will vary. The girls will most likely maintain a relationship with their mother since Delphine references a letter Cecile writes to her a month later. The girls might return to Oakland for another visit since they have established friendships with many people and now have a relationship with Cecile. The girls' relationship with Big Ma might change since they now believe they should assert their rights as individuals and as young black women, instead of always being polite and well-behaved. They may also be less inclined to allow Big Ma to speak negatively about Cecile.)*

Post-reading Extension Activities

Writing

1. Write a back-to-school essay entitled "My Summer Vacation" from Delphine's, Vonetta's, or Fern's point of view.
2. Write a poem of at least 15 lines about a modern-day issue that you care about (e.g., the environment, poverty, racism).
3. Create an award for this novel. Write a speech you would give when presenting the award to the author.
4. Write a letter to the author describing your feelings about the novel.
5. From Delphine's point of view, write a response to the letter Cecile wrote a month after their visit.

Art

6. Illustrate three similes or metaphors from the novel, and explain what they mean.
7. Research the fashions inspired by the 1960's Civil Rights Movement. Learn how the desire to show black pride and a connection to African roots influenced how a number of African Americans dressed at the time. Sketch articles of clothing inspired by this era.

Speaking/Drama

8. Pretend you are a television reporter from Brooklyn interviewing the Gaither girls about the rally for Bobby Hutton. Perform the interview for the class.
9. Find a poem by a female poet from the 1960s (e.g., Sonia Sanchez, Gwendolyn Brooks, Nikki Giovanni, June Jordan, Lucille Clifton), and recite the poem for the class.

Social Studies

10. A number of important events occurred in America in 1968. Research these events, and complete the Time Line on page 32 of this guide.
11. Interview someone who remembers the 1960s. What are his or her memories and impressions from the Civil Rights Movement?
12. Research the Black Panthers, and determine 1) whether they were a violent or peaceful organization and 2) what their goal was.

Assessment for *One Crazy Summer*

Assessment is an ongoing process. The following ten items can be completed during study of the novel. Once finished, the student and teacher will check the work. Points may be added to indicate the level of understanding.

Name ______________________________ Date ____________

Student	Teacher	
______	______	1. Working in a small group, write five review questions about your assigned section. Participate in an oral review.
______	______	2. Complete the Bio-poem on page 33 of this guide for your favorite character from the novel.
______	______	3. In a small group, make flash cards using the vocabulary words and take turns quizzing one another.
______	______	4. Write a book review. Include a short summary of the novel along with your recommendation for the novel.
______	______	5. Compare two of your completed Post-reading Extension Activities with members of a small group.
______	______	6. Complete the Story Map on page 34 of this guide.
______	______	7. Revise one of the paragraphs you wrote as a Supplementary Activity.
______	______	8. Use the Venn Diagram on page 35 of this guide to compare and contrast two characters from the novel.
______	______	9. Complete the following sentence, and explain your response in a short paragraph. "Something I know now that I didn't know before I read this novel is ______________________."
______	______	10. Correct all quizzes taken over the novel.

I Have Heard of…

A. Directions: Tell whether you are familiar with each of the following people, events, or cultural trends of the 1960s by placing a checkmark in the appropriate column.

	Yes	No
Civil Rights Movement	____	____
Martin Luther King, Jr.	____	____
Black Panthers	____	____
Huey Newton	____	____
Bobby Hutton	____	____
hippies	____	____
flower children	____	____
Black Power	____	____
Gwendolyn Brooks	____	____
Lyndon B. Johnson	____	____
the Vietnam War	____	____
Afros	____	____
Cassius Clay	____	____

B. Directions: Now, choose one of the topics above that you have heard of. On the lines below, write what you know about the chosen topic. Share your knowledge with the class.

____

____

____

____

____

____

____

____

____

____

____

____

I Predict...

Directions: Spend a few minutes looking at the cover of the novel and flipping through its pages. What can you predict about the characters, the setting, and the problem in the novel? Write your predictions in the spaces below.

The Characters	The Setting	The Problem

From the information you gathered above, do you think you will enjoy reading this novel? Circle your response on the scale below.

0 —— 1 —— 2 —— 3 —— 4 —— 5 —— 6 —— 7 —— 8 —— 9 —— 10

I will not like this novel. I will really like this novel.

Explain your prediction on the lines below.

Word Map

Synonyms

Magazine cut-out, drawing, or symbol that shows what the word means

Word

Definition in your own words

Word used in a sentence

First-Person Narration

Advantages	Disadvantages

Time Line

Directions: In the numbered boxes below, write four main events from 1968 in the order they occurred. In the larger boxes, describe the significance of each event.

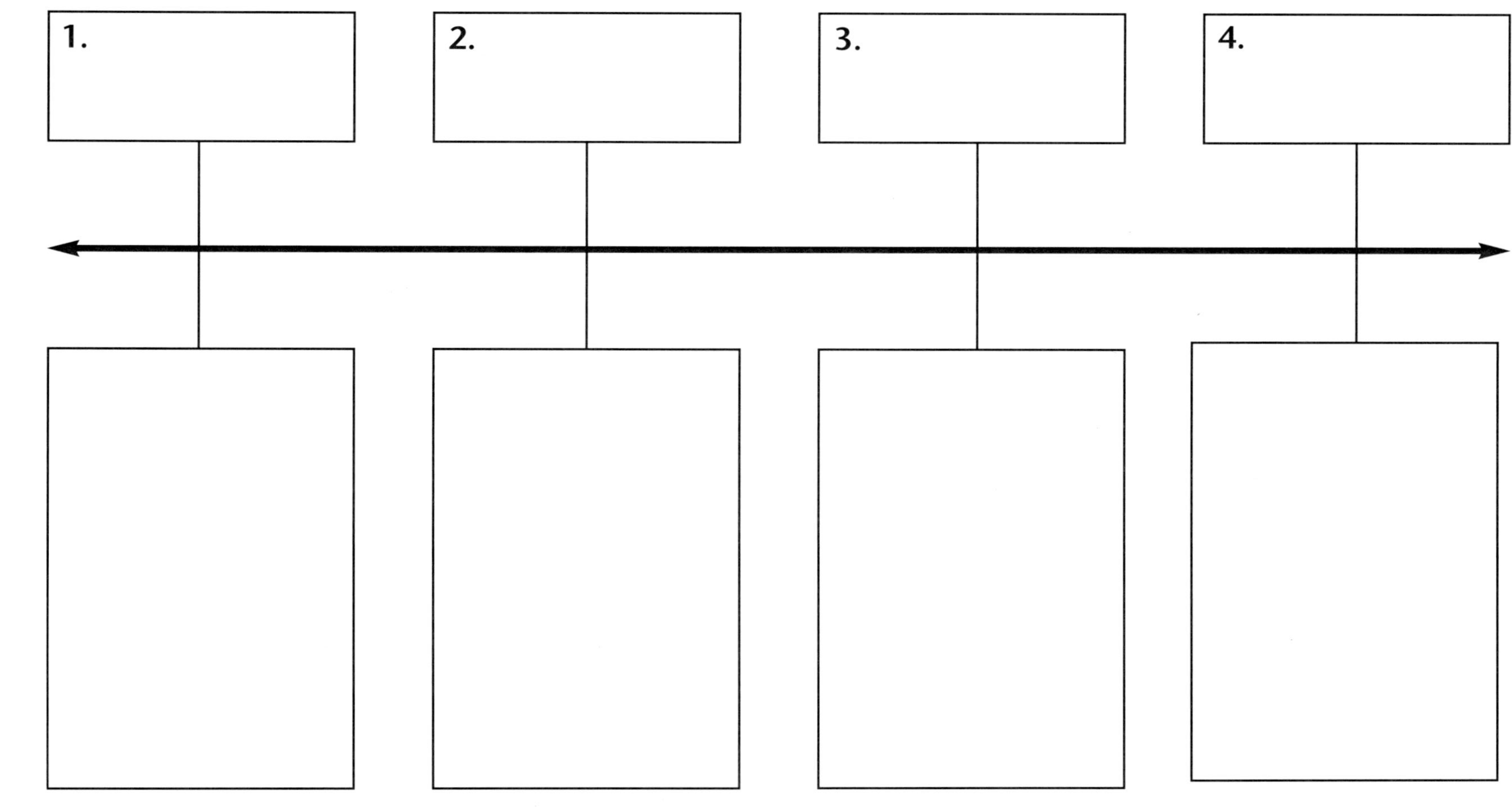

Bio-poem

Directions: Using the format below, write a bio-poem about a main character in the novel. Then, write a bio-poem about yourself using the same format. Write a paragraph describing the values and characteristics you share.

—Line 1: First name only
—Line 2: Lover of (list three things character loves)
—Line 3: Giver of (list three things character gives)
—Line 4: Needs (list three things character needs)
—Line 5: Wants (list three things character wants)
—Line 6: Is good at (list three things character is good at)
—Line 7: Should work on (list three things character needs to improve)
—Line 8: Is similar to (list three people or other characters to whom this character is similar and list a reason behind each character)
—Line 9: Survivor of (list three things the character survives)
—Line 10: Last name only

Title ______________________________

1. ____
2. ____
3. ____
4. ____
5. ____
6. ____
7. ____
8. ____
9. ____
10. ____

Story Map

Directions: Complete the story map below.

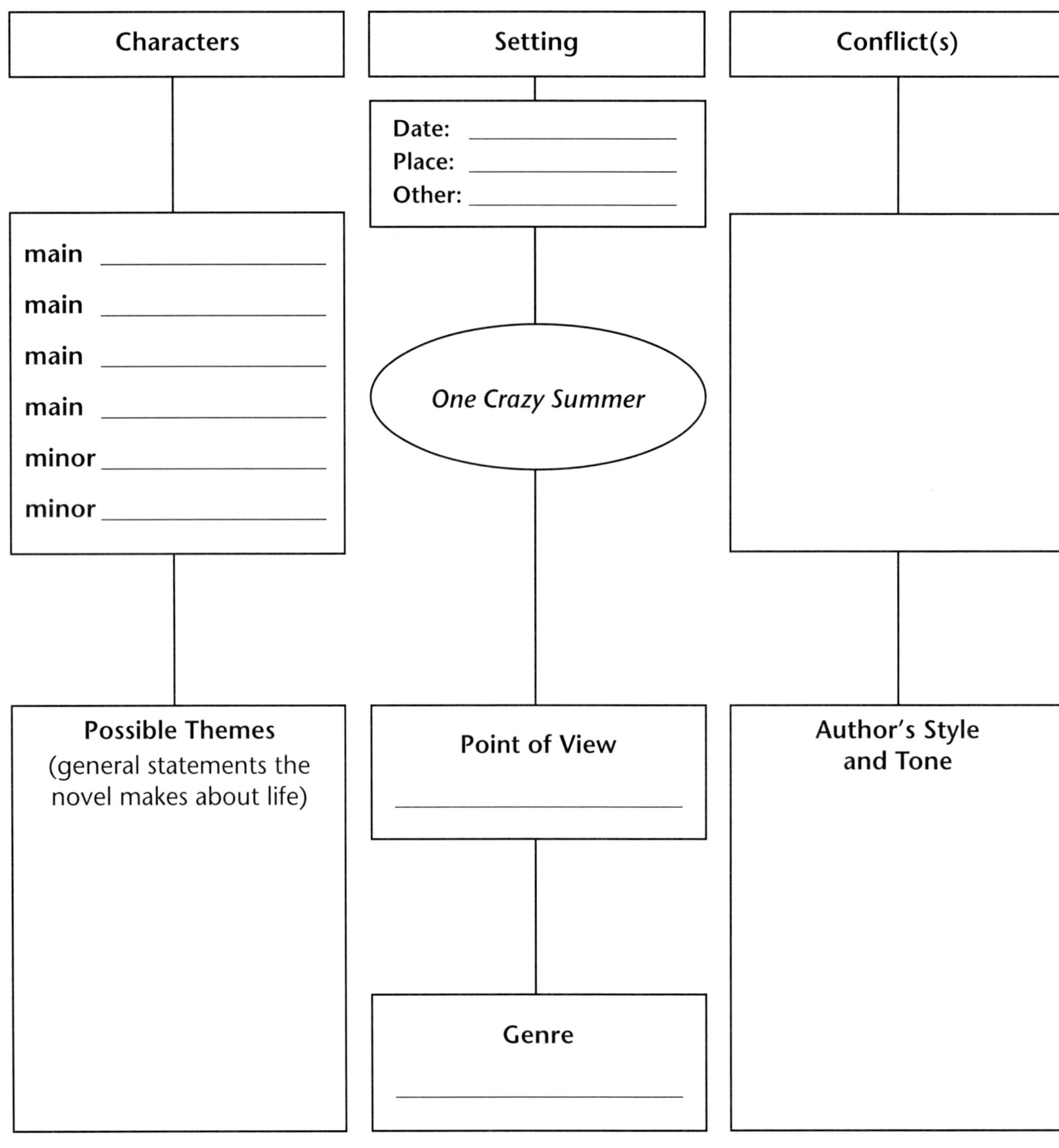

Venn Diagram

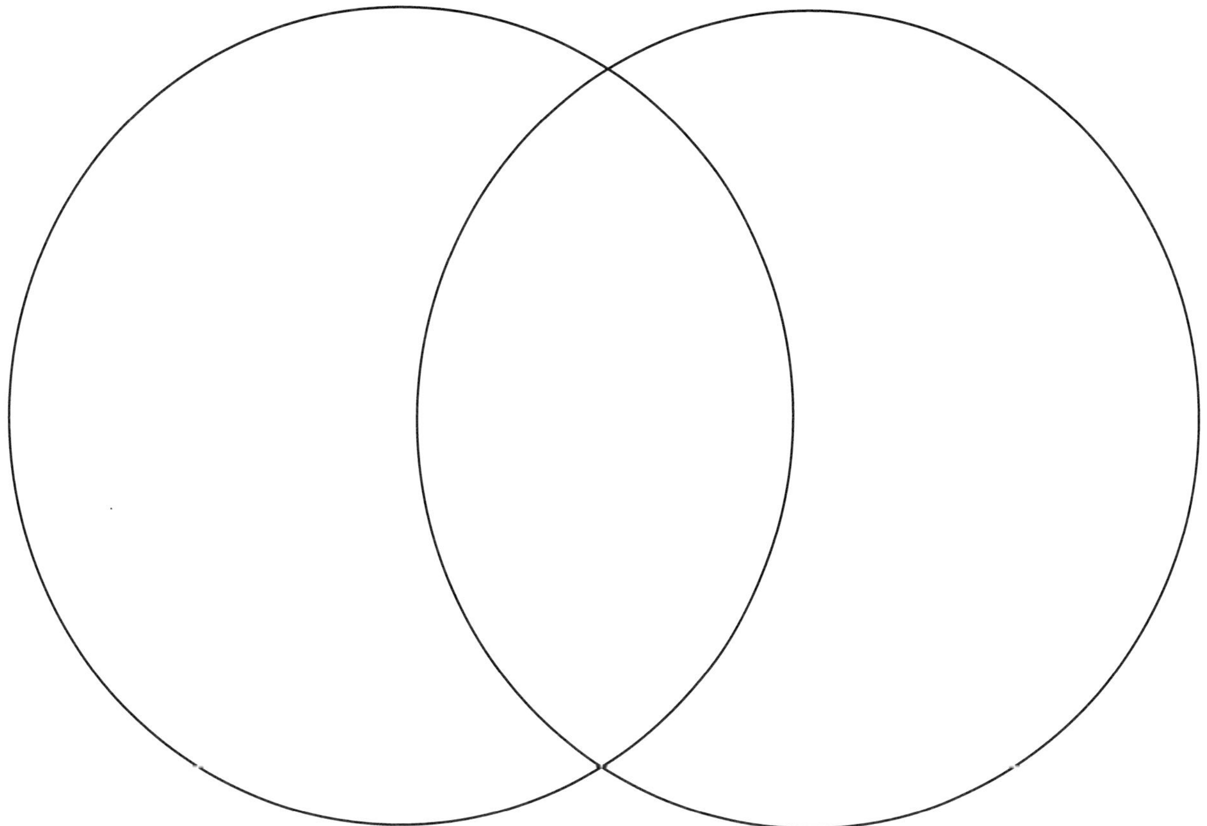

Linking Novel Units® Lessons to National and State Reading Assessments

During the past several years, an increasing number of students have faced some form of state-mandated competency testing in reading. Many states now administer state-developed assessments to measure the skills and knowledge emphasized in their particular reading curriculum. The discussion questions and post-reading questions in this Novel Units® Teacher Guide make excellent open-ended comprehension questions and may be used throughout the daily lessons as practice activities. The rubric below provides important information for evaluating responses to open-ended comprehension questions. Teachers may also use scoring rubrics provided for their own state's competency test.

Please note: The Novel Units® Student Packet contains optional open-ended questions in a format similar to many national and state reading assessments.

Scoring Rubric for Open-Ended Items

3-Exemplary	Thorough, complete ideas/information Clear organization throughout Logical reasoning/conclusions Thorough understanding of reading task Accurate, complete response
2-Sufficient	Many relevant ideas/pieces of information Clear organization throughout most of response Minor problems in logical reasoning/conclusions General understanding of reading task Generally accurate and complete response
1-Partially Sufficient	Minimally relevant ideas/information Obvious gaps in organization Obvious problems in logical reasoning/conclusions Minimal understanding of reading task Inaccuracies/incomplete response
0-Insufficient	Irrelevant ideas/information No coherent organization Major problems in logical reasoning/conclusions Little or no understanding of reading task Generally inaccurate/incomplete response